Curé of Ars

Prayer Book

FAMILY PUBLICATIONS · OXFORD

© Family Publications 2009

All pictures © Sanctuaire d'Ars,
Clichés Danièlle Bouteaud and Stéphane Gorret

Texts from the writings of St John Vianney

The Little Catechism of the Curé of Ars © St Meinrad's Abbey, 1951
and
Thoughts of the Curé D'Ars © Burns & Oates, 1967
Reproduced by kind permission of
Continuum International Publishing Group

Papal texts © Libreria Editrice Vaticana

ISBN 978-1-871217-94-0

published by
Family Publications
Denis Riches House
66 Sandford Lane, Kennington
Oxford, OX1 5RP
www.familypublications.co.uk

printed in England
through s|s|media ltd

Table of Contents

Introduction 5
Prayer in the Life of St John Vianney 6
The Christian Life 9
Daily Offering 11
The Sacred Heart 13
The Priest 15
How Great is a Priest 17
Sin 19
Grace 21
Listening to the Word of God 23
Confession 25
The Mass 27
The Eucharist 29
Communion 31
The Real Presence 33
Eucharistic Adoration 35
Prayer 37
The Heart of Mary 39
Mary Our Intercessor 41
Prayer for Vocations 43
Prayer for Seminarians 45
Prayer for Priests 47
Prayer for my Parish Priest 49
Prayer to St John Vianney for a holy death 51
Prayer Before the Crucifix 53
On Faith, Hope and Charity 55
Prayer for Parish Priests 57
Act of Love of St John Vianney 59
Litany in Honour of St John Vianney 61
Indulgences 64

*J*ean-Marie Vianney was born near Lyons in 1786 and from an early age wanted to become a priest. After his ordination in 1815, he was sent to the little village of Ars where he was parish priest for forty-one years and was noted for his great devotion to the Eucharist. His spiritual direction soon attracted growing numbers of pilgrims who came to him in Ars for Confession and to listen to his religious instructions. He died in 1859, aged 73. Canonised in 1925 by Pope Pius XI, he was declared the Patron of all parish priests. His feast day is 4 August. He is now one of our most popular saints.

Thinking of priests in love with the Eucharist, we cannot forget St John Mary Vianney, the humble parish priest of Ars … With the holiness of his life and his pastoral zeal, he succeeded in making that little village a model Christian community, enlivened by the Word of God and by the Sacraments.

Pope Benedict XVI
18 September 2005

Introduction

*W*e live in a difficult time for the Church, and perhaps particularly for priests. It isn't only the scandals, which have been painful enough. Even more, perhaps, it is the crisis of the rapid decline in the number of priests, and the various attempts being made as a result to manage parishes to optimum effect. With this has gone a certain devaluation of the role of the priest in the Church.

The 'Year for Priests' beginning on June 19th this year and including the 150th anniversary of the death of St Jean-Marie Vianney on August 4th, is a wonderful opportunity both for priests and people to recover a truer perspective. The contemplation of the texts offered in this little book, and the praying of its prayers, will surely be a real help to this.

It is not simply a matter of returning to priests the status they may once have enjoyed, still less an inflation of it. Some of the language employed in these texts might imply this. 'Everything has come to us through the priest'; 'after God, the priest is everything'. But in fact, no one could be less self-important than the Curé of Ars. Indeed he refused all honours, and sold his canon's robes for the benefit of the poor.

What shines through language which may sometimes seem exaggerated, and indeed is necessarily of its time, is the priest as instrument of the grace and mercy of the living God, through Word and Sacrament and prayer, touching and transforming souls.

Fr Paul King
Our Lady of the Rosary Parish
Hinksey, Oxford

Prayer in the Life of St John Vianney

Pope John XXIII

*H*ow timely and how profitable this example of constant prayer on the part of a man completely dedicated to caring for the needs of souls is for priests in Our own day, who are likely to attribute too much to the effectiveness of external activity and stand ready and eager to immerse themselves in the hustle and bustle of the ministry, to their own spiritual detriment!

"The thing that keeps us priests from gaining sanctity" – the Curé of Ars used to say – "is thoughtlessness. It annoys us to turn our minds away from external affairs; we don't know what we really ought to do. What we need is deep reflection, together with prayer and an intimate union with God." The testimony of his life makes it clear that he always remained devoted to his prayers and that not even the duty of hearing confessions or any other pastoral office could cause him to neglect them. Even in the midst of tremendous labours, he never let up on his conversation with God.

But listen to his own words; for he seemed to have an inexhaustible supply of them whenever he talked about the happiness or the advantages that he found in prayer: "We are beggars who must ask God for everything"; "How many people we can call back to God by our prayers!" And he used to say over and over again: "Ardent prayer addressed to God: this is man's greatest happiness on earth!"

And he enjoyed this happiness abundantly when his mind rose with the help of heavenly light to contemplate the things of heaven and his pure and simple soul rose with all its deepest love from the mystery of the Incarnation to the heights of the Most Holy Trinity. And the crowds of pilgrims who surrounded him in the temple could feel something coming forth from the depths of the inner life of this humble priest when words like these burst forth from his inflamed breast, as they often did: "To be loved by God, to be joined to God, to walk before God, to live for God: O blessed life, O blessed death!"

Sacerdotii Nostri Primordia, 36–39
1 August 1959

The parish church and the basilica in Ars.

All our religion is but a false religion, and all our virtues are mere illusions and we ourselves are only hypocrites in the sight of God, if we have not that universal charity for everyone — for the good, and for the bad, for the poor and for the rich, and for all those who do us harm as much as for those who do us good.

The Christian Life

There are many Christians who do not even know why they are in the world. "Oh my God, why hast Thou sent me into the world?" "To save your soul." "And why dost Thou wish me to be saved?" "Because I love you." The good God has created us and sent us into the world because He loves us; He wishes to save us because He loves us. . . . To be saved, we must know, love and serve God. Oh, what a beautiful life! How good, how great a thing it is to know, to love and serve God! We have nothing else to do in this world. All that we do besides is lost time. We must act only for God, and put our works into His hands. . . . We should say, on awaking, "I desire to do everything today for Thee, O my God! I will submit to all that Thou shalt send me, as coming from Thee. I offer myself as a sacrifice to Thee. But, O God, I can do nothing without Thee. Do Thou help me!"

Father of mercy, you made St John Vianney outstanding in his priestly zeal and concern for your people. By his example and prayers, enable us to win our brothers and sisters to the love of Christ and come with them to eternal glory. We ask this through our Lord Jesus Christ, your Son, who lives and reigns with you and the Holy Spirit, one God, for ever and ever.

Amen.

St John Vianney's room in the presbytery of Ars.

" *Oh! how I love those words said the first thing in the morning: I will do and suffer everything this day for the Glory of God ... nothing for the world or personal interest, all to please my Saviour!* "

Daily Offering

*A*t the beginning of the day, I endeavour to unite myself closely with Jesus Christ, and then I do the next thing, with the thought of this union in mind.

In your work, offer your difficulties and troubles quite simply to God ... and you will find that his blessing will rest upon you and on all you do.

We ought in the morning on awaking to offer to God our heart, our mind, our thoughts, our words, our actions, our whole selves, to serve for his glory alone.

Receive, O my God, all my thoughts and all I am going to do today, in union with all you bore out of love for me during your life on earth.

*F*ather, I offer to you all my thoughts, words, and deeds today. Show me how to find you in everything. Let me see that you are active in my life.

I offer you all my sufferings and whatever hardship I may meet along the way.

Whatever I do, may it be for your glory alone.

Amen.

On the feast of the Sacred Heart, Our Lord places us on His Heart. Ah! if we could remain there always.

The Sacred Heart

*G*od contemplates a pure soul with love; He grants it all it desires. How could He refuse anything to a soul that lives only for Him, by Him, and in Him? It seeks God, and He shows Himself to it; it calls Him, and God comes; it is one with Him; it captivates His will. A pure soul is all-powerful with the gracious Heart of Our Lord. A pure soul with God is like a child with its mother. It caresses her, it embraces her, and its mother returns its caresses and embraces.

O Blessed Jean-Marie, pray for us; obtain that we may walk in Jesus' train with that faith, hope and charity which opened to you the Heart of the Divine Master and the treasury of His graces.

*M*ay Thy holy mysteries, O Lord Jesus, produce in us a divine fervour, whereby, having tasted the sweetness of Thy most dear Heart, we may learn to despise earthly things and love those of heaven.

Amen.

A chasuble worn by St John Vianney.

"Do not try to please everybody. Try to please God, the angels, and the saints – they are your public."

The Priest

◆

*S*t Bernard tells us that everything has come to us through Mary; and we may also say that everything has come to us through the priest; yes, all happiness, all graces, all heavenly gifts. If we had not the Sacrament of Orders, we should not have Our Lord. Who placed Him there, in that tabernacle? It was the priest. Who was it that received your soul, on its entrance into life? The priest. Who nourishes it, to give it strength to make its pilgrimage? The priest. Who will prepare it to appear before God, by washing that soul, for the last time, in the blood of Jesus Christ? The priest – always the priest. And if that soul comes to the point of death, who will raise it up, who will restore it to calmness and peace? Again the priest. You cannot recall one single blessing from God without finding, side by side with this recollection, the image of the priest.

*L*ord, we give thanks for priests who bring You to us. We give thanks for all the graces and gifts we have received through their ministry during our lives. Grant us holy priests, entirely devoted to the service of souls, in teaching the faith and ministering the Sacraments, so that we may be led to your heavenly Kingdom.

Amen.

*The priesthood is the love of the Heart of Jesus.
When you see the priest,
think of our Lord Jesus Christ.*

How great is a Priest

Oh, how great is a priest! The priest will not understand the greatness of his office till he is in Heaven. If he understood it on earth, he would die, not of fear, but of love. The other benefits of God would be of no avail to us without the priest. What would be the use of a house full of gold, if you had nobody to open you the door! The priest has the key of the heavenly treasures; it is he who opens the door; he is the steward of the good God, the distributor of His wealth. Without the priest, the Death and Passion of Our Lord would be of no avail. Look at the heathens: what has it availed them that Our Lord has died? Alas! they can have no share in the blessings of Redemption, while they have no priests to apply His Blood to their souls!

The priest is not a priest for himself; he does not give himself absolution; he does not administer the Sacraments to himself. He is not for himself, he is for you. After God, the priest is everything.

God Our Father, we thank you for all our parish priests. We entrust them to your paternal care. Help them in the challenges and difficulties they are faced with. Guide them in their ministry, and keep them faithful to their calling as pastors of your flock and stewards of your Kingdom.

Amen.

The chapel of La Providence in Ars.

With the Name of Jesus we shall overthrow the demons; we shall put them to flight. With this Name, if they dare to attack us, our battles will be victories.

Sin

*S*in is the executioner of the good God, and the assassin of the soul. It snatches us away from Heaven to precipitate us into Hell. And we love it! What folly! If we thought seriously about it, we should have such a lively horror of sin that we could not commit it. O my children, how ungrateful we are! The good God wishes to make us happy; that is very certain; He gave us His Law for no other end. The Law of God is great; it is broad. King David said that he found his delight in it, and that it was a treasure more precious to him than the greatest riches. He said also that he walked at large, because he had sought after the Commandments of the Lord. The good God wishes, then, to make us happy, and we do not wish to be so. We turn away from Him, and give ourselves to the devil! We fly from our Friend, and we seek after our murderer! We commit sin; we plunge ourselves into the mire. Once sunk in this mire, we know not how to get out. If our fortune were in the case, we should soon find out how to get out of the difficulty; but because it only concerns our soul, we stay where we are.

*F*ather, open our eyes and our hearts to see our sin. Give us, we pray, the grace to overcome the root of our sin. Turn us from the snares of the Devil, from self-will and from pride. May we too know your Divine Mercy, so that, bathed in your forgiveness, we may hear your voice calling us to be with you in Paradise.

Amen.

The basilica of Ars.

As the earth can produce nothing unless it is fertilised by the sun, so we can do no good without the grace of the good God.

Grace

All our merit, my children, consists in cooperating with grace. See, my children, a beautiful flower has no beauty nor brilliancy without the sun; for during the night it is all withered and drooping. When the sun rises in the morning, it suddenly revives and expands. It is the same with our soul, in regard to Jesus Christ, the true Sun of justice; it has no interior beauty but through sanctifying grace. In order to receive this grace, my children, our soul must turn to the good God by a sincere conversion: we must open our hearts to Him by an act of faith and love. As the sun alone cannot make a flower expand if it is already dead, so the grace of the good God cannot bring us back to life if we will not abandon sin.

Lord Jesus, sun of justice, shine upon our souls, so that we may be brought back to life. Help your faithful turn from sin and receive the grace of your Spirit. Through the merits and prayers of St John Vianney, grant us, we pray, a share in the life of the Most Holy Trinity.

Amen.

The pulpit in the parish church in Ars.

The priest is the instrument that the Good God makes use of to distribute His holy Word.

You pour liquor through a funnel; whether it be made of gold or of copper, if the liquor is good, it will still be good.

Listing to the Word of God

Listening to the Word of God

⌒

*M*y children, the Word of God is of no little importance!
These were Our Lord's first words to His Apostles:
"Go and teach" … to show us that instruction is before
everything.

My children, what has taught us our religion? The
instructions we have heard. What gives us a horror of sin?
What makes us alive to the beauty of virtue, inspires us
with the desire of Heaven? Instructions. What teaches
fathers and mothers the duties they have to fulfill towards
their children, and children the duties they have to fulfill
towards their parents? Instructions.

*S*t John Vianney, pray that we may hear the Word of God,
listen to God's will, and grow in faith. Teach us to treasure
the Divine Word, revealed through the Church.

We ask your intercession for preachers, so that, following
your example, their words may inspire the minds and
move the hearts of God's people and lead them to His
eternal glory.

Amen.

St John Vianney's confessional.

"Our faults are like a grain of sand beside the great mountain of the mercies of the good God."

Confession

*G*o to confession to the Blessed Virgin, or to an angel; will they absolve you? No. Will they give you the Body and Blood of Our Lord? No. The Holy Virgin cannot make her Divine Son descend into the Host. You might have two hundred angels there, but they could not absolve you. A priest, however simple he may be, can do it; he can say to you, "Go in peace; I pardon you."

Remember that when the priest gives you absolution, you have but one thing to think of – that the Blood of the good God is flowing over your soul to purify it and make it as bright as it was made by its Baptism.

God makes greater speed to pardon a penitent sinner than a mother to snatch her child out of the fire.

*L*ord God, we thank you for the beauty and grace of the Sacrament of Reconciliation. Give us deeper faith in the power of this sacrament to purify and renew our soul, and grant us greater confidence in your boundless mercy.

Amen.

St John's chalice.

"*Holy Communion and offering the Holy Sacrifice ... are the two most powerful means of intercession for others' conversion.*"

The Mass

After the Consecration, when I hold in my hands the most holy Body of Our Lord, and when I am in discouragement, seeing myself worthy of nothing but Hell, I say to myself, "Ah, if I could at least take Him with me! Hell would be sweet with Him; I could be content to remain suffering there for all eternity, if we were together. But then there would be no more Hell; the flames of love would extinguish those of justice." How beautiful it is. After the Consecration, the good God is there as He is in Heaven. If man well understood this mystery, he would die of love.

Lord, we thank you for the beauty of the mystery of the Mass, given to us in your Holy Church.

We thank you for sending us priests to act in the person of your beloved Son, and to offer the most Holy Sacrifice of the Mass.

We bring you our prayers and intentions to be united to the Sacrifice of the altar. We praise and thank you.

Amen.

Benediction with a monstrance used by St John Vianney.

O! if we could rightly understand how Jesus Christ loves to come into our heart!

The Eucharist

*W*ithout the Holy Eucharist there would be no happiness in this world; life would be insupportable. When we receive Holy Communion, we receive our joy and our happiness. The good God, wishing to give Himself to us in the Sacrament of His love, gave us a vast and great desire, which He alone can satisfy. In the presence of this beautiful Sacrament, we are like a person dying of thirst by the side of a river – he would only need to bend his head; like a person still remaining poor, close to a great treasure – he need only stretch out his hand. He who communicates loses himself in God like a drop of water in the ocean. They can no more be separated.

*D*ear Jesus, we thank you for the joy and happiness brought to us by the Most Holy Eucharist.

Come and slake our thirst, satisfy our hunger.

Deepen our desire to receive you in this Sacrament of your Love, so that we might become one with you for ever.

Amen.

A modern icon of St John Vianney.

" *It is only God that can fill the soul.* "

Communion

I do not like people to begin to read directly when they come from the holy table. Oh no! what is the use of the words of men when God is speaking? We must do as one who is very curious, and listens at the door. We must listen to all that God says at the door of our heart. When you have received Our Lord, you feel your soul purified, because it bathes itself in the love of God. When we go to Holy Communion, we feel something extraordinary, a comfort which pervades the whole body, and penetrates to the extremities. What is this comfort? It is Our Lord, who communicates Himself to all parts of our bodies, and makes them thrill. We are obliged to say, like St John, "It is the Lord!" Those who feel absolutely nothing are very much to be pitied.

*M*y Lord and my God,
  I thank you for coming to me in the Most Holy Sacrament. Dwell in me, fill my soul, vivify me, and sustain me in the pilgrimage of life. As I become more conformed to your image and united to you, enable me to draw others to your Mystical Body, the Church.

Amen.

*The tabernacle in the parish church in Ars
before which St John spent many hours in prayer.*

*We know that God is there
in His holy tabernacle;
let us open our hearts to Him;
let us rejoice in His Presence:
this is the best prayer.*

The Real Presence

*O*ur Lord is hidden there, waiting for us to come and visit Him, and make our request to Him... He is there to console us; and therefore we ought often to visit Him. How pleasing to Him is the short quarter of an hour that we steal from our occupations, from something of no use, to come and pray to Him, to visit Him, to console Him for all the outrages He receives! ... What happiness do we not feel in the presence of God, when we find ourselves alone at His feet before the holy tabernacles! ... Ah! If we had the eyes of angels with which to see Our Lord Jesus Christ, who is here present on this altar, and who is looking at us, how we should love Him! We should never more wish to part from Him. We should wish to remain always at His feet; it would be a foretaste of Heaven: all else would become insipid to us. But see, it is faith we want. We are poor blind people; we have a mist before our eyes. Faith alone can dispel this mist. Presently, my children, when I shall hold Our Lord in my hands, when the good God blesses you, ask Him then to open the eyes of your heart; say to Him like the blind man of Jericho, "O Lord, make me to see!" If you say to Him sincerely, "Make me to see!" you will certainly obtain what you desire, because He wishes nothing but your happiness.

O Jesus, we thank you for your presence in the tabernacle. We believe in you, but increase our faith so that we may rejoice in your presence always. Open our hearts and our eyes, so that what we see now by faith, we may one day see in glory

Amen.

We should consider those moments spent before the Blessed Sacrament as the happiest of our lives.

Eucharistic Adoration

When we are before the Blessed Sacrament, instead of looking about, let us shut our eyes and our mouth; let us open our heart: our good God will open His; we shall go to Him, He will come to us, the one to ask, the other to receive; it will be like a breath from one to the other. What sweetness do we not find in forgetting ourselves in order to seek God! The saints lost sight of themselves that they might see nothing but God, and labour for Him alone; they forgot all created objects in order to find Him alone. This is the way to reach Heaven.

My Dear Jesus,
I adore you in the Most Holy Sacrament of the Eucharist.
I adore and praise your Most Holy Name.
I adore and worship your Body hidden in the Sacrament.
I adore your humility in veiling your Godhead.
I adore your Most Sacred Heart masked by these shadows.
I adore for ever the Most Holy Sacrament.

Amen.

*We do not have
to talk very much
in order to pray well.*

Prayer

*P*rayer is a fragrant dew; but we must pray with a pure heart to feel this dew. There flows from prayer a delicious sweetness like the juice of very ripe grapes. Prayer disengages our soul from matter; it raises it on high, like the fire that inflates a balloon.

The more we pray, the more we wish to pray. Like a fish which at first swims on the surface of the water, and afterwards plunges down, and is always going deeper, the soul plunges, dives, and loses itself in the sweetness of conversing with God. Time never seems long in prayer. I know not whether we can even wish for Heaven? Oh, yes! ... The fish swimming in a little rivulet is well off, because it is in its element; but it is still better in the sea. When we pray, we should open our heart to God, like a fish when it sees the wave coming. The good God has no need of us. He commands us to pray only because He wills our happiness, and our happiness can be found only in prayer. When He sees us coming, He bends His heart down very low towards His little creature, as a father bends down to listen to his little child when it speaks to him.

*A*lmighty and merciful God who didst bestow upon St John Mary wonderful pastoral zeal and a great fervour for prayer and penance, grant we beseech thee, that by his example and intercession we may be able to gain the souls of our brethren for Christ, and with them attain everlasting glory, through the same Christ our Lord.

Amen.

Statue of Our Lady in the parish church in Ars.

If you invoke the Blessed Virgin when you are tempted, she will come at once to your help, and Satan will leave you.

The Heart of Mary

The Father takes pleasure in looking upon the heart of the most Holy Virgin Mary, as the masterpiece of His hands; for we always like our own work, especially when it is well done. The Son takes pleasure in it as the heart of His Mother, the source from which He drew the Blood that has ransomed us; the Holy Ghost as His temple. The Prophets published the glory of Mary before her birth; they compared her to the sun. Indeed, the apparition of the Holy Virgin may well be compared to a beautiful gleam of sun on a foggy day.

The greater sinners we are, the more tenderness and compassion does she feel for us. The child that has cost its mother most tears is the dearest to her heart. Does not a mother always run to the help of the weakest and the most exposed to danger? Is not a physician in the hospital most attentive to those who are most seriously ill? The Heart of Mary is so tender towards us that those of all the mothers in the world put together are like a piece of ice in comparison to hers.

O Mary, Mother of the Church, we come to you as your children. Come to our aid when we are tempted, show us your compassion and motherly tenderness when we fall by the wayside, and lead us to the Redemption wrought by your Son Jesus Christ.

Amen.

Statue of Our Lady placed outside the parish church in 1844.

Happy is he who lives and dies under the protection of the Blessed Virgin.

Mary Our Intercessor

*W*hen we have to offer anything to a great personage, we get it presented by the person he likes best, in order that the homage may be agreeable to him. So our prayers have quite a different sort of merit when they are presented by the Blessed Virgin, because she is the only creature who has never offended God. The Blessed Virgin alone has fulfilled the first Commandment – to adore God only, and love Him perfectly. She fulfilled it completely.

All that the Son asks of the Father is granted Him. All that the Mother asks of the Son is in like manner granted to her. When we have handled something fragrant, our hands perfume whatever they touch: let our prayers pass through the hands of the Holy Virgin; she will perfume them. I think that at the end of the world the Blessed Virgin will be very tranquil; but while the world lasts, we drag her in all directions. … The Holy Virgin is like a mother who has a great many children – she is continually occupied in going from one to the other.

O Blessed Virgin, Mother of God, teach us to adore your Son and to love Him perfectly as you did. We bring to you all our intentions so that you may present them to your beloved Son. We entrust particularly to your maternal care all those who are dear to us, and especially all the priests of the Church.

Amen.

A monument to commemorate the meeting between a young shepherd and the curé of Ars arriving at his new parish.

" *You have shown me the way to Ars, I will show you the way to heaven.* "

Prayer for Vocations

*W*e ask the eternal Father that the memory of the Curé of Ars may help to stir up our zeal in his service. We beseech the Holy Spirit to call to the Church's service many priests of the calibre and holiness of the Curé of Ars: in our age she has so great a need of them, and she is no less capable of bringing such vocations to full flower. And we entrust our Priesthood to the Virgin Mary, the Mother of priests, to whom John Mary Vianney ceaselessly had recourse with tender affection and total confidence. This was for him another reason for giving thanks: "Jesus Christ," he said, "having given us all that he could give us, also wishes to make us heirs of what is most precious to him, his holy Mother."

Pope John Paul II,
Letter To All the Priests of the Church
for Holy Thursday 1986

*M*y Dear Jesus,

Thou desirest that we pray the Lord of the Harvest that He send zealous labourers into His harvest. Deign to raise up in Thy Church, and especially in this diocese, numerous and holy priests who, taking Thy Divine Heart as their Model, will, in the exercise of their holy priesthood, promote the glory of Thy heavenly Father and the salvation of those souls whom Thou hast redeemed with Thy Precious Blood.

Give us truly holy priests who, inflamed with the fire of Thy divine love, seek nothing but Thy greater glory and the salvation of souls.

O Mary, Queen of the clergy, pray for us; obtain for us a great number of vocations to the holy priesthood.

Amen.

God has given each of us our own work to do. It is for us to pursue our road, that is to say, our vocation. ... When God gives us such and such a vocation, he bestows upon us at the same time his grace to fulfil it.

Prayer for Seminarians

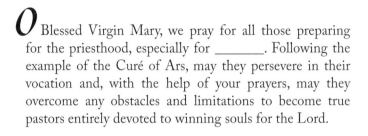

O Blessed Virgin Mary, we pray for all those preparing for the priesthood, especially for _____. Following the example of the Curé of Ars, may they persevere in their vocation and, with the help of your prayers, may they overcome any obstacles and limitations to become true pastors entirely devoted to winning souls for the Lord.

Amen.

*S*t John Vianney, we ask your prayers for all the seminarians in this country. Enkindle in them a burning zeal for souls and ardour for the Faith.

May they find in you a template of perseverance and love of the Church.

Pray, we ask, for all those preparing for ordination; may you be an encouragement for them.

Be an example to them of prayer, service, and a love of the Sacraments.

Amen.

A side chapel in the basilica of Ars containing the casket with the incorrupt body of St John Vianney.

"*One ought to pray earnestly that God will give us good priests. If they are saints, what good they are able to do!*"

Prayer for Priests

~

*O*h, how great is a priest! if he understood himself he would die ... God obeys him; he speaks two words and Our Lord comes down from Heaven at his voice, and shuts Himself up in a little Host. God looks upon the altar. "That is My well-beloved Son", He says, "in whom I am well-pleased." He can refuse nothing to the merits of the offering of this Victim. If we had faith, we could see God hidden in the priest like a light behind a glass, like wine mingled with water.

*S*aintly Pastor of Ars and outstanding model of all servants of souls, you were at one time considered unsuited to the priesthood, but you possessed the wisdom of the Saints. You were a true conveyor of God's mercy to his people as countless penitents streamed to your confessional. Inspire priests in our day to speak Christ's words of forgiveness to his people, and to lead them to their eternal home.

Amen.

The beginning of a celebration in Ars.

" *A saint has told us that one day at Mass he saw Jesus Christ with his hands full of gifts, looking for souls to whom he might give them.* "

Prayer for my Parish Priest
(to be said daily)

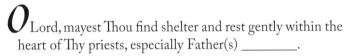

O Lord, mayest Thou find shelter and rest gently within the heart of Thy priests, especially Father(s) _____ .

Make them, O Lord, priests according to Thy heart: meek, humble, zealous, so that all they do will be for Thine honour and glory.

Mould them into men of prayer and labour, insensible to earthly things, and sensible only to Thy love and to the graces of the Holy Ghost.

Amen.

S t John Vianney, Curé of Ars, pray for the Church, that we might learn your love of the Eucharist and find example in your pastoral zeal.

Set on fire with the love of God, you are a model of holiness and virtue; may we learn from your simple wisdom.

Martyr of the confessional, you are an example of patience, sacrifice and tenderness; may we be inspired by your witness to the Faith.

Amen.

PRAECLARI · EXEMPLI · PATRONO · GALLIARVM · SACERDOTES

The incorrupt body of Saint John Vianney in the basilica of Ars.

O my children! What folly is the world! We come into it, we go out of it, without knowing why. The good God places us in it to serve Him, to try if we will love Him and be faithful to His law.

Life is given us that we may learn to die well, and we never think of it.

Prayer to St John Vianney for a holy death

A day will come, perhaps it is not far off, when we must bid adieu to life, adieu to the world, adieu to our relations, adieu to our friends. When shall we return, my children? Never. We appear upon this earth, we disappear, and we return no more; our poor body, that we take such care of, goes away into dust, and our soul, all trembling, goes to appear before the good God. When we quit this world, where we shall appear no more, when our last breath of life escapes, and we say our last adieu, we shall wish to have passed our life in solitude, in the depths of a desert, far from the world and its pleasures. We have these examples of repentance before our eyes every day, my children, and we remain always the same. We pass our life gaily, without ever troubling ourselves about eternity. By our indifference to the service of the good God, one would think we were never going to die.

*S*t John Vianney, pastor of immortal souls, your eyes were set on heaven.

May we not be forgetful of our mortal condition on earth.

Teach us detachment from worldly gains and goods.

Show us the path to true life and happiness.

May we have the graces of repentance and final perseverance at the hour of our death.

Pray for us in our last moments, we beseech you.

Amen.

The crucifix from the high altar in St John's parish church in Ars.

O what inspiration there is in the Crucifix! Who could find it hard to persevere at the sight of a God who never commands us to do anything which he has not first practised himself?

Prayer Before the Crucifix

~

When we offend the good God, if we were to look at our crucifix, we should hear Our Lord saying to us in the depths of our soul, "Wilt thou too, then, take the side of My enemies? Wilt thou crucify Me afresh?" Cast your eyes on Our Lord fastened to the Cross, and say to yourself, "That is what it cost my Saviour to repair the injury my sins have done to God!" A God coming down to earth to be the victim of our sins, a God suffering, a God dying, a God enduring every torment, because He would bear the weight of our crimes! At the sight of the Cross, let us understand the malice of sin, and the hatred we ought to feel for it. Let us enter into ourselves; let us see what we can do to make amends for our poor life.

My loving Jesus, I adore you in your most Sacred Passion. I am truly sorry for my sin which has crucified you. Imprint in my soul your divine love. Hide me in your wounds. Wash me in the water flowing from your side. Cleanse me in your Most Precious Blood. Purify my soul.

Amen.

Ex-votos and crutches in a chapel in the parish church of Ars.

Prayer is the source of all graces, the mother of all virtues, the efficacious and universal way by which God wills that we should come to Him.

On Faith, Hope and Charity

*M*y children, the three acts of faith, hope and charity contain all the happiness of man upon the earth. By faith, we believe what God has promised us: we believe that we shall one day see Him, that we shall possess Him, that we shall be eternally happy with Him in Heaven. By hope, we expect the fulfilment of these promises: we hope that we shall be rewarded for all our good actions, for all our good thoughts, for all our good desires; for God takes into account even our good desires. What more do we want to make us happy?

In Heaven, faith and hope will exist no more, for the mist which obscures our reason will be dispelled; our mind will be able to understand the things that are hidden from it here below. We shall no longer hope for anything, because we shall have everything. We do not hope to acquire a treasure which we already possess. . . . But love; oh, we shall be inebriated with it! we shall be drowned, lost in that ocean of divine love, annihilated in that immense charity of the Heart of Jesus! so that charity is a foretaste of Heaven. Oh, how happy should we be if we knew how to understand it, to feel it, to taste it! What makes us unhappy is that we do not love God.

O Jesus, fill our hearts with the virtues of Faith, Hope and Charity. Above all, help us grow in Charity so that we may, one day, finally be plunged in the ocean of your Divine Love.

Amen.

*The chapel of La Providence in Ars where
St John would give instructions.*

An old peasant went into the church every
day before going to work, and again on his
return. 'Père Chaffangeon, what do you say
to Our Lord, during your visits?' asked M.
Vianney. 'I say nothing to him, M. le Curé,
I look at him and he looks at me'.

Prayer for Parish Priests

*D*ear Saint John Vianney, your childhood dream was to be a priest, to win souls for God. You endured years of toil and humiliation to attain the Priesthood. You became a priest truly after God's own heart, outstanding in humility and poverty, prayer and mortification; totally devoted to the service of God's people. The Church has exalted you as model and patron saint of all Parish Priests, trusting that your example and prayers will help them to live up to the high dignity of their vocation to be faithful servants of God's people, to be perfect imitators of Christ the Saviour who came not to be served but to serve, to give His Life in ransom for many.

Pray that God may give to His Church today many more priests after His own Heart. Pray for all the priests under your patronage, that they may be worthy representatives of Christ the Good Shepherd. May they wholeheartedly devote themselves to prayer and penance; be examples of humility and poverty; shining models of holiness; tireless and powerful preachers of the Word of God; zealous dispensers of God's Grace in the Sacraments. May their loving devotion to Jesus in the Eucharist and to Mary His Mother be the twin fountains of fruitfulness for their ministry.

Amen.

St John Vianney in prayer by Cabuchet.

Act of Love of St John Vianney

I love You, O my God, and my sole desire is to love You until the last breath of my life.

I love You, O infinitely lovable God, and I prefer to die loving You than live one instant without loving You.

I love You, O my God, and I do not desire anything but heaven so as to have the joy of loving You perfectly.

I love You, O my God, and I fear hell, because there will not be the sweet consolation of loving You.

O my God, if my tongue cannot say in every moment that I love You, I want my heart to say it in every beat. Allow me the grace to suffer loving You, to love you suffering, and one day to die loving You and feeling that I love You. And as I approach my end, I beg you to increase and perfect my love of You.

Amen.

The chapel with the shrine containing the heart of St John Vianney.

Litany in Honour of St John Vianney

Lord, have mercy. Lord, have mercy.

Christ, have mercy. Christ, have mercy.

Lord, have mercy. Lord, have mercy.

Christ, hear us. Christ, graciously hear us.

God the Father of Heaven, have mercy on us.

God the Son, Redeemer of the world, have mercy on us.

God the Holy Ghost, have mercy on us.

Holy Trinity, One God, have mercy on us.

Holy Mary, Mother of God, pray for us.

Saint John Vianney, pray for us.

St John Vianney, endowed with grace from your infancy, pray for us.

St John Vianney, model of filial piety, pray for us.

St John Vianney, devoted servant of the Immaculate Heart of Mary, pray for us.

St John Vianney, spotless lily of purity, pray for us.

St John Vianney, faithful imitator of the sufferings of Christ, pray for us.

St John Vianney, abyss of humility, pray for us.

St John Vianney, seraph of prayer, pray for us.

St John Vianney, faithful adorer of the Most Blessed Sacrament, pray for us.

St John Vianney, ardent lover of holy poverty, pray for us.

St John Vianney, true son of St Francis of Assisi, pray for us.

St John Vianney, exemplary Franciscan tertiary, pray for us.

St John Vianney, tender friend of the poor, pray for us.

St John Vianney, penetrated with the fear of God's judgment, pray for us.

St John Vianney, fortified by divine visions, pray for us.

St John Vianney, who was tormented by the evil spirit,
    pray for us.
St John Vianney, perfect model of sacerdotal virtue, pray for us.
St John Vianney, firm and prudent pastor, pray for us.
St John Vianney, inflamed with zeal, pray for us.
St John Vianney, faithful attendant on the sick, pray for us.
St John Vianney, indefatigable catechist, pray for us.
St John Vianney, who did preach in words of fire, pray for us.
St John Vianney, wise director of souls, pray for us.
St John Vianney, specially gifted with the spirit of counsel,
    pray for us.
St John Vianney, enlightened by light from Heaven, pray for us.
St John Vianney, formidable to Satan, pray for us.
St John Vianney, compassionate with every misery, pray for us.
St John Vianney, providence of the orphans, pray for us.
St John Vianney, favoured with the gift of miracles, pray for us.
St John Vianney, who did reconcile so many sinners to God,
    pray for us.
St John Vianney, who did confirm so many of the just in the way
    of virtue, pray for us.
St John Vianney, who did taste the sweetness of death,
    pray for us.
St John Vianney, who now rejoices in the glory of Heaven,
    pray for us.
St John Vianney, who gives joy to those who invoke you,
    pray for us.
St John Vianney, heavenly patron of parish priests, pray for us.
St John Vianney, model and patron of directors of souls,
    pray for us.
Lamb of God, Who takes away the sins of the world,
    spare us, O Lord.
Lamb of God, Who takes away the sins of the world,
    graciously hear us, O Lord.

Lamb of God, Who takes away the sins of the world,
   have mercy on us.
Christ, hear us. Christ, graciously hear us.

℣. Pray for us, Saint John Vianney,
℟. That we may be made worthy of the promises of Christ.

Let Us Pray

   Almighty and merciful God, Who did bestow upon blessed
   John Vianney wonderful pastoral zeal and a great fervour
   for prayer and penance, grant, we beseech You, that by his
   example and intercession we may be able to gain the souls of
   our brethren for Christ, and with them attain to everlasting
   glory, through the same Jesus Christ Your Son our Lord, Who
   lives and reigns with You and the Holy Spirit, one God, for
   ever and ever.

                                                    Amen.

Indulgences

During the special Year for Priests – 19 June 2009 to 19 June 2010 – on the occasion of the 150th anniversary of St John Vianney's death, indulgences may be obtained when meeting the following conditions:

A plenary indulgence for priests

who, on any day, devoutly recite at least Lauds or Vespers before the Blessed Sacrament, exposed for public adoration or in the tabernacle, and who offer themselves with a ready and generous heart for the celebration of the sacraments, especially Confession

when they receive sacramental Confession and the Eucharistic banquet and pray for the Pope's intentions

A plenary indulgence for the lay faithful

on the first and last days of the special Year, as well as on St John Vianney's feast day (August 4), and on the first Thursday of each month

when attending Mass, offering prayers to Jesus Christ the Eternal High Priest for the priests of the Church, going to sacramental Confession, and praying for the intentions of the Pope

A partial indulgence for the lay faithful

every time they devoutly recite five Our Fathers, Hail Marys and Glory Bes, or another expressly approved prayer, in honour of the Sacred Heart of Jesus, to obtain that priests be preserved in purity and holiness of life.